by Jarrett Mentink, Ph.D.
Illustrated by Patrick Carlson

This book is dedicated to all of those parents who help their kids to fly!

Printed in Korea, First Edition.
ISBN: 0-9723314-2-5

Published by Kids in the Clouds™
www.kidsintheclouds.com

Baseball has history,
hot streaks and slumps,
Stretches and mascots,
and strike calling umps.

And if you know baseball,

you may know the name Boone –

And if not, just read on,

you will very soon!

There once was a Boone

with a furry pelt hat.

But our Boone isn't Daniel –

He works with a bat!

He plays second base

for the M's of the West.

Bret is his name,

and he's one of the best!

His skills are amazing,

and he's tough at the plate.

But there's something more special

that makes Boonie so great.

It's the fact he remembers

the lessons each day

That he learned from his father

and his beloved Grandpa Ray.

Three Boone generations

to play major league ball –

The first family in history

to answer this call!

This spectacular trio

of Bret, Bob, and Ray

Gave baseball new meaning

to the term triple play!

Bret put to good use

his Boone family ears,

Listening to those

who had played ball for years.

They taught him the tools

and tricks of the trade,

And respect for the way

the game should be played.

Boonie worked hard
from tee ball on up.
He played with the zeal
of a newborn pup!

For Bret loved the game

with his heart and his soul.

So much, he once played

nearby the North Pole!

It was a team in Alaska

called the Fairbanks Goldpanners.

Bret was praised for his play

And of course his good manners!

At every stop,

Boone honed his skills.

Now this proud Mariner

fills Safeco with thrills!

He plays some on grass

and plays some on dirt –

And likes nothing more

than stains on his shirt.

LAUNDRY - $2.00

For that probably means
he's been diving about,
Making great plays
to throw runners out.

He can go up the middle

or deep in the hole.

It seems with his range

that his glove's on a pole.

One thing that helps Boonie

make wonderful plays

Is the fact he can throw

in so many ways.

He can toss it real soft,

or fire it hard –

Skills that he learned

playing in his backyard.

If he's down on a knee

there's no need to worry.

He can sling it sidearm

to first in a hurry.

Some even say

he can throw on his back

While sipping a soda

or eating a snack.

He takes base hits away

and makes hot hitters cold,

Which is why our good Boonie

has gloves made of gold!

One thing's for certain,

if you see his bat flip,

Boone's sent the ball

to the moon on a trip!

Perhaps you recall back

in 2001,

Bret and the M's

had a whole lot of fun!

Boonie went wild,

with 141 RBI's.

He Hit .331

and had 37 Big Flies!

But the best part of all,

was that the fans exchanged grins,

As he helped the team tie

the all-time record for wins!

He's great in the field,

he's great at the dish.

In the world of baseball,

he's a mighty big fish!

But as good as he is,

at the end of the day,

Bret thanks his pops

and his Grandfather Ray.

For they passed on to Boonie

the words of the wise,

And grateful is Bret

for his strong family ties.

So take Bret's advice
and learn something each day.
Then share it with others
and show them the way!

Written by Jarrett Mentink, Ph.D.
Illustrated by Patrick Carlson